Exploring God

Exploring God

Group study course based on the Communion
with photocopiable resources

Andrew & Elizabeth Procter

kevin
mayhew

First published in 2003 by

KEVIN MAYHEW LTD
Buxhall, Stowmarket, Suffolk IP14 3BW
E-mail: info@kevinmayhewltd.com

KINGSGATE PUBLISHING INC
1000 Pannell Street, Suite G, Columbia, MO 65201
E-mail: sales@kingsgatepublishing.com

9 8 7 6 5 4 3 2 1 0

ISBN 1 84417 058 6
Catalogue No. 1500581

Cover design by Jonathan Stroulger
Edited by Elisabeth Bates
Typesetting by Richard Weaver

Printed and bound in Great Britain

Contents

To Cathy,
our tireless church office secretary who worked so hard,
so often and at such short notice to make our
Exploring God courses happen.

Introduction – Explorers

Have you ever wondered about explorers? Have you thought that they were crazy people setting off to find something most people didn't care about and pushing themselves to and beyond the limits of human endurance? To explore means to go out beyond, to break new territory, to search out something just because it is there. This desire to find out, to conquer and know is embedded deep within the human spirit. There is an excitement in breaking new ground. There is a fear of the unknown, the testing of one's reserves of courage and endurance, the buzz that comes from adrenaline, and the deep satisfaction of finding. For most of us we are content to let others do this rather than set off ourselves, or we explore locally in small bits! We regard the true explorers and adventurers as eccentric and foolhardy.

Their folly sometimes cost them a great deal. For some, like Scott, it cost them their lives. Why did they do it? Always it was deeply expensive, so somehow it must have felt worthwhile. There was no doubt a whole range of motives . . . fame, riches, a place in history, an act of faith.

For Celtic Christians like Columba, exploring was part of a faith journey, a commitment to being part of a pilgrim people. Columba set sail from Ireland in a coracle without oars, abandoning himself, as an act of faith, to where God, or the current, wind and tides would take him. He arrived in Iona in 563.

Marco Polo was a trader and merchant who travelled overland to China in 1260 in search of spices and with the trade he became rich. His book, *The Travels of Marco Polo*, is perhaps the most famous and influential travel book in history. With a wealth of vivid detail, it gave medieval Europe its first consequential knowledge of China and its first information concerning other Asian countries. The book became the basis for some of the first accurate maps of Asia made in Europe. It helped to arouse in Christopher Columbus an interest in the Orient. Based on information acquired during his travels, and by reading and studying charts and maps, Christopher Columbus concluded that the earth was 25 per cent smaller than was previously thought, and composed mostly of land.

On the basis of these faulty beliefs, he decided that Asia could be reached more quickly by sailing west rather than east. He eventually persuaded and received backing from Spain and so set sail in 1492. He arrived at various islands in the West Indies and although he made three further voyages he never managed to reach Asia.

The desire for fame and glory for the British Empire drove Scott to embark on a second Antarctic expedition in 1910, with the aim of being the first man to reach the South Pole. He landed at McMurdo Sound and with four companions began a trek of 1842 miles, the longest continuous sledge journey ever made in the Polar Regions. Scott reached the South Pole on January 18, 1912, only to find the tent and flag of the Norwegian explorer Roald Amundsen, who had achieved the goal five weeks earlier. The return journey ended in the loss of the entire party.

The desire to conquer nature spurred Edmund Hillary to join the British Mount Everest Expedition in 1953 as one of the chief climbers. Hillary reached the summit on May 29, 1953, and was knighted for the achievement later that year. These are a few of the better known explorers of this globe, driven by many different desires.

What about exploration for the Christian believer? Jesus said, 'I am the door' (John 10:7), and claimed, 'I am the way the truth and the life' (John 14:6). Often Christian believers know how to get in the door, to find their way into the sheepfold. They know that putting their faith and hope in Jesus Christ alone will set them on the Way, but then what? A cutting critique of contemporary Christianity in a church newspaper suggested that modern Christians get inside the door, but stand around in the porch. They are very good at checking that others are coming in the right way, but totally neglect to investigate and explore where they have found themselves, to seek out and search the vastness of the God with whom they now relate. It is as though they are satisfied with finding a safe place. But God is not safe. He is wild and untamed – 'the Lion of the tribe of Judah' (Revelation 5:5), unknown and he calls us ever deeper into himself and his heart. Like Abraham we are called to set out in faith on a journey, not knowing where we are going, nor how we are going to get there, but to keep pressing on in. Ezekiel gives us a picture of the river flowing from the throne of God (Ezekiel 47:3-5). We are to wade into it until we are out of our depth, a scary place yet a secure one, held in the vastness of God.

Plainly, no single course can explore the whole of God. We will need to set some parameters. God is a vast and unknown 'world'. We cannot do more than begin on one 'continent' in that world. This course makes a start on exploring the 'continent' of God indwelling us. The journey to the centre of oneself to find God is one that has excited and challenged Christians throughout history. Much of John's writing refers to God's indwelling (John 14:16-15:8; 17:22-23; 1 John 4:12-16) and Paul too writes of 'Christ in you, the hope of glory' (Colossians 1:27). Jesus encourages believers to recognise that within themselves are lifesprings of God – 'out of his heart shall flow streams of life-giving water' (John 7:37) – and says, 'If anyone hears my voice and opens the door, I will come in and eat with him and he with me' (Revelation 3:20). Hence this particular journey of exploration is inward, to explore God as he dwells within us. This is a valuable and valid journey. Many revered Christians of previous generations have sought to explore God in this way. St Theresa of Avila wrote that St Augustine sought God in many places and at last found the Almighty within himself. Theresa herself wrote about this journeying inward in *The Interior Castle.* More recently a contemporary writer, Margaret Silf, picks up this idea in *Landmarks* and writes of an inner journey whereby the immanent God (the God who is within us) and the transcendent God (he who is totally other) meet and we feel 'touched by God'. Rowan Williams writes of the journey 'to the place where God's love meets and mingles with the life of the soul' (Theresa of Avila). So the main thrust of this *Exploring God* course is an inward exploration of the God within us.

And once we look inside ourselves, what do we find? In our experience, both in our personal exploring God and in helping others to do so, there is enormous unsearched terrain, in memory and life experience, of God's presence already there within us. It has often gone unacknowledged, unappreciated and unexplored. Jesus says, 'the Kingdom of God is within you' (Luke 17:21). Often we feel ignorant of God and inexperienced about God. We feel the need to go to something outside of ourselves to meet God properly, when all along

God has been revealing himself in our day-to-day experience and waiting to be explored there. This course is designed to help people discover God's active living presence in their own lives.

Some will ask how does this inner journey differ from self-analysis and navel-gazing? Is our subjective experience of God valid? But how else are we to know God except through experiencing him via our human make-up and consciousness? Perhaps we need to keep in mind that it is God whom we seek in this inner exploration? If we become more absorbed in our own inner workings than in finding him, we are likely to go astray. Some self-knowledge is important and can help us see where God is at work within, but it is only a means to an end, that end being our God and gazing on him. The value of the group experience of exploring is that other group members are able to authenticate our individual experience. Also, to ensure that we do not get too absorbed with ourselves and our experiences, each session involves looking at some part of the Christian experience which is outside ourselves. This is most often a look at a Bible passage, but at other times we look at nature, Christian history, even at newspapers. From them we will be able to glean insights about God which we can cross-reference with our individual experience.

We also ground this exploration firmly in the Christian tradition. A great fear that many have when exploring is that of becoming totally lost, confused and bewildered, adrift with no bearings or landmarks. We have set the map for exploration as the most common pattern for Christian worship, the central theme of a Holy Communion/Lord's Supper/Eucharist: around the centrality of the Cross and the sacrificial death of Jesus Christ.

In seeking to explore the vastness of God we have many guides. We are privileged to live two millennia after Christ. We are not the first explorers. The course is a synthesis or blend of many types of Christian spirituality. It gives a taster of different approaches and hopefully will surprise and delight the searcher in finding new routes, new terrain to explore. It gives a simple set of tools, or kit with which to start. But it is vital to remember that each journey is unique. Explorers don't necessarily tread in one another's footsteps. In fact the essence of exploration is to branch out into something new, unknown, untested and untried. Therefore what follows are only pointers and waymarks of the general direction to go in. One can dally, come off the main route, play at the roadside or venture into neighbouring fields to see what is there. To act as safeguards or landmarks in exploration will be pointers from strands of well-tried and tested spirituality, which are both authentic and traditional but possibly novel to the explorer. Some will excite and beckon, others will not appeal. Try, taste, explore. The safe and comfortable route is rarely the way of God (Matthew 7:14). God's vastness is not constrained within one approach; rather it may reveal a single facet of his glory. There will be many, many more to find and explore – and that is the challenge: to explore the unknown God who is there.

Imagine seeing the sky from a town with tall buildings. True it is the sky, but the magnitude and the span are dulled from that perspective. Or only viewing the sky by day and not by night means that one never appreciates the billions of stars out beyond our world. How different the sky looks from a hillside or clifftop, how much more vast and awe-inspiring. This is what we hope *Exploring God* will do. Give an opportunity to gaze on the vastness of God from a new and different place.

The explorer will be encouraged to use all five senses during the sessions and in the short pieces of homework they will be asked to do. There will be some imaginative Bible study and reading. These link largely with Ignatian spirituality. There will be an introduction to the use of silence and reflection and recollection along the lines of contemplative spirituality. There will be touches of Celtic spirituality in the awareness of God in the ordinary daily life and the here and now. Use is made of the group experience and people are encouraged to develop their inner creativity, often with surprising results and excitement for themselves and a deepening awareness of God. The course incorporates music and art, candles and food, and allows for sharing of serious things as well as laughter. And it is sacramental. It does not pretend to be all embracing, but perhaps gives the explorer a way into new landscapes, an encouragement to push on further into the unknown to wider horizons.

Andrew and Elizabeth Procter

Planning and Preparation

Most expeditions of exploration involve a great deal of preparation. Indeed it is likely that the preparation will take longer than the expedition itself. With the Fiennes/Stroud expedition to Antarctica, for instance, there were two years of preparation for a journey lasting 97 days.

And it is not the mere length of the preparations but their thoroughness that is important. The entire venture will stand or fall by the depth of work going into the preparations. Equipment needs to be gathered, maybe even designed. It needs to be tested or it could give way at a vital time far from help or possibility of repair. Foresight and planning are needed. It is no good only seeing as far as the first few stages of the journey. The thing needs to have been thought through right to its ending as well. Possible snags need to be anticipated as far as possible, allowance needs to be made for many variables, which could make or break the endeavour.

It is the same with *Exploring God.* Running a course rewards some thoughtful and thorough preparation. Much of this preparation would apply to running any group study course and we will leave general matters of forward planning to people's common sense. We will take it as understood that the group's ethos will be one of mutual upbuilding, where each person's contribution is regarded as an unquestionably valid gift to the group, where criticism or correction have no place, where a loving acceptance is paramount.

Otherwise, suffice it to mention here those areas of preparation which are special to *Exploring God* and which tend not to have to be done when doing a more usual group study.

We think it helps *Exploring God* group members enormously if they can **arrive to a period of quiet meditation**, usually best backed by music, at the start of group sessions. This helps them to be relaxed, sloughing off the other concerns of their day before things begin. It also gives time to still themselves, being more prepared to open themselves to God and to others. So it is important to have a good room well prepared, with music facilities, for this to be possible.

Another less usual feature of *Exploring God* sessions is the use of **a central table** as a focus for the group's thinking throughout. This need be no more than a coffee table with interesting centrepieces designed to aid group members' exploration of God. Simple things like an attractive cross, an icon, pebbles, shells, candles, flowers, pottery, a small piece of driftwood, blossom, autumn leaves – the sky is the limit really. Having such a thing as a visual focus is surprisingly nourishing, adding to the value of the group's life. It is good, too, to vary the table's contents a little from session to session to give a sense of flow to the course. Also the course guidance notes rely on using the table in certain ways from time to time. So it is important to have it well prepared in advance of the first arrivals, session by session. We have usually placed an empty Communion plate and cup on the table at the first five sessions to help create the sense of an extended communion service. This may be an option you choose.

A third particular feature of *Exploring God* is **the Holy Communion** element. The introduction has explained that the whole course is structured as an extended communion service. This brings with it a need for good forward planning. It will be important to anticipate the ultimate celebration of the Holy Communion at the final session. You may need a minister to join you or at least secure ministerial permission. You may have denominational differences to consider. You may need already to be thinking about the form your celebration will take, though our guidance notes on it suggest only the simplest of formats. You may want to be thinking right from the outset about what participation, if any, in the final celebration your different group members might best make.

Another particular element in the course is the **hometask** for group members between sessions. These are an invaluable aid to deepening the lasting impact of the course in people's lives. They also help link one session to the next, both consolidating the previous session and preparing for the forthcoming one. We strongly recommend including them in your leadership of the course and, incidentally, doing the tasks yourselves!

Yet another thing in *Exploring God* is the commitment group members make to **spend 10 minutes per day** in silent prayer. This we suggest you treat lightly but seriously. The point of it is to furnish a kind of seedbed of receptivity in group members to what God reveals of himself during the course and also to build up a pattern of daily silent prayer which we hope remains after the course is over. We stress that this prayer need not be in addition to people's existing disciplines of prayer, but can be taken into it. We also stress that where people find they are not doing very well at it, that is accepted (whereas with the hometasks it matters if it's not done). Also if people are feeling they do not concentrate well in the silence, do reassure them that this is normal: it seems to be the offering of oneself that matters most rather than any sense of composure.

It is worth a word about **music** in the group. How much any group uses music needs to be left open to its particular needs and preferences. We do suggest every group uses music as a background to the opening 20 minutes of arrivals. We do not make any suggestions as to what type of music to use. There is such an easily available and wide choice of classical and modern, sacred and secular that it does not seem necessary. We also recommend every group tries to sing at the final Holy Communion and we put in something to this effect in the guidance notes. There just seems to be something so special at these times, in our experience, that it is worth even the least musical of groups trying to offer praise in this way. Beyond that – some groups will revel in singing together or using music in some other way, others will not. We leave it to you.

As another special feature of *Exploring God* we offer at the end of this chapter a list of **recommended reading**. These are manageable extracts from mainstream Christian works on the themes of the respective sessions. They are no more than an optional suggestion. They are designed to supply affirmation to course members that the course material connects with wider Christian thought and also to give them the chance of deepening their appreciation of the subject areas covered. Some groups will be more literate than others and some group members will be more literate than others. It is up to you whether to use it or not. Obviously, if you do, there will be the need to address getting hold of copies of the relevant books and making arrangements for their distribution.

We do include also, for use in the opening session, a **Contract.** This sets agreed standards for the group on such things as attendance, punctuality, confidentiality and commitment to the hometasks. We have found it a useful tool for setting up good expectations in our groups and its terms have always been readily agreed. We appreciate it may seem a little officious to some and would not wish to press its use, but, on the whole, we recommend it.

Lastly, we do recommend that you try to make *Exploring God* feel special to group members in a number of small ways. The aim is to mark being on the course as something above and beyond the routine church study group experience. By giving attention to some relatively small details it is possible to heighten people's expectations of the course, and to encourage them to attach a high value to it and so derive its full benefit. We refer to such details as having individually named and prepared folders ready for each member at the first session; having the right number of seats pleasantly arranged around the central table; having an attractive notice on the door inviting people in and good coat-hanging facilities so they can enter the room for the opening quiet period without fuss. We find that keeping precise timings for opening and closing sessions relieves a lot of anxiety and promotes focused involvement in the group's life. Giving thought to things like lighting and heating can make a big difference, and perhaps to have rather superior biscuits for the refreshments. In short aim to foster the understanding that you regard your members and the course as special, so that they are lifted up in spirit to do the same.

Lastly, a word about the course's overall structure: we have designed the course based on six sessions held at a fortnightly frequency in the evenings. We hope it is sufficiently flexible to adapt to other patterns than this – different lengths of course and times to meet are perfectly possible. Similarly, we have given timings in our course guidance notes based on sessions lasting 90 minutes, finding this the best for us. Here again, we hope our material proves adaptable for those preferring a shorter or longer time. We have ended up limiting the size of our groups to a minimum of four (excluding us two) and a maximum of ten. These have seemed the parameters best for us: but, again, we hope those wanting to work with more or less group members can adapt. As to leadership for the course: we have been able to work as a married couple in joint leadership always. We tend to think that some form of shared leadership is preferable to someone working alone. This is because then you are able as leaders to compare notes on how the group is doing. We find that usually group members need sensitive and skilful handling and two heads are better than one.

And so – thus prepared – on to the course itself. God speed you in your exploring!

Recommended reading

We include some recommended reading around the course's themes. This is meant to be a voluntary helpful extra for group members. We want to stress that the course is not an academic one. The reading is only voluntary, designed as a help to those who like reading. You might like to give some thought to seeing if you can come by a pool of the books and extracts indicated. They are very mainstream. You and your members may well already have some copies between yourselves. Failing that your church bookstall/library may help. Facilitating this might even be a useful thing to delegate to a group member with the energy for it.

Session One

Come Let Us Play! **Wanda Nash** (Darton, Longman & Todd, London, 1999).

This book is good for an overall feel of the ethos *Exploring God* aims for.

Landmarks, **Margaret Silf** (Darton, Longman & Todd, London, 1998), pp. 31-43.

This is a very good chapter about exploring the inner self to find our 'Godseed'.

Session Two

Listening to Others, **Joyce Huggett** (Hodder & Stoughton, London, 1988), pp. 102-107.

This is a very useful look at the art of true listening.

Session Three

The Way of an Intercessor, **Audrey Merwood** (Kingsway, Eastbourne, 1985).

Session Four

Doubt, **Os Guinness** (Lion Publishing, Berkhamsted, 1976), pp. 229-230.

Session Five
Enfolded in Love – Daily Readings with Julian of Norwich
(Darton, Longman & Todd, London, 1994).

These are wonderful short meditations with a particular grace in the area of our fallibility and forgiveness.

The Expedition

Session One: Almighty God

Outline programme

7.40pm-8pm	Arrivals.
8pm-8.10pm	Exercise on what it feels like to be here.
8.10pm-8.40pm	Introduction to the Course: a. Overall concept; b. Structure and shape, framework, contract, folders and materials.
8.40pm-8.45pm	Opening of communion service and collect for purity.
8.45pm-9.15pm	Exercise: Ten minutes to consider and jot down up to three experiences of God's might, followed by time of sharing just one of these with the group.
9.15pm-9.30pm	God's might as Creator (Isaiah 40:22-26). Hometask explained to group.
9.30pm	Ends.

Guidance notes for leaders

Aim of Session

The aim of this first session is to welcome everyone, to set course expectations and to break the ice. The theme is 'Almighty God' and in this session we explore together people's experiences of God's might within their own lives.

Preparation in advance

- The **room** in which you hold course sessions.
- The **central table** which is a focal point for sessions, plus a Communion plate and cup (optional).
- **Music** both for the opening 20-minute arrivals time and for during the sessions.
- The **recommended reading**, if you are using it, and how you will help people to come by it.
- The **folders** for each group member to have throughout the course.

Things you will need in order to lead the first session in particular are:

- Individual copies of a list of all **group members' names and phone numbers**.
- Individual copies of a list of **times, dates and venues** of all course sessions.
- Enough copies of the **Contract (Handout 1A)**.
- A **named folder** for each group member.
- Some **spare pens and writing paper**.
- Your **Bible**, ready to read from Isaiah chapter 40 and some **spare Bibles** for those who have forgotten theirs.
- Enough individual copies of the **Hometask (Handout 1B)** to be done for Session Two.
- Copies of the **Prayer of Preparation** (if you chose to have it written).

7.40pm-8pm **Arrivals**

As we have explained in 'Planning and Preparation', please have your meeting room ready for the group members to arrive at any time from 20 minutes before the formal time onwards. Have your background music playing. Have any candles lit, and the central table arranged.

8pm-8.10pm **Exercise on what it feels like to be here**

Start promptly, even if not everyone has arrived. This sets up an expectation of a good disciplined approach to the course.

Welcome everyone. You may like to do a round of introductions on their own or you may prefer to subsume this into the first exercise. This will probably depend on how much your members already know each other. We find just a round of names can be rather bald. People will pretty soon get to know each other. Inevitably, it will all feel a little stiff at first. Don't worry about this. They won't properly relax until next session.

As the exercise, ask people to say what it feels like to be there in the room. Either do this as a round of the circle or, perhaps better, let people speak as and when they wish. Don't allow any discussion of what people share. Simply let it be absorbed by the group. You might try the odd follow up question. Otherwise thank people for their contributions and move on. A variant on this is to ask people simply to share one word only, which most describes their feelings on being there.

You will learn a great deal from this, of course. Log people in your mind. Try to form an impression of why they have come, who is reluctant, who is outgoing, who is retiring and so on.

8.10pm-8.40pm **Introduction to the Course**

Structure and shape, framework, the Contract, folders and materials

This section is designed to help them get their bearings as quickly as possible.

Pass round the **folders containing the lists of course members and of times, dates and venues of meetings, and the Contract**. (Nothing more just yet.) Make sure that all the details are correct and that people are happy with arrangements. Are there any queries? If so, answer them as best you can.

Then move on to **the Contract** (if you have chosen to use it). Run through it with the group. See if they are happy to accept it as it stands. It has always seemed reasonable to members of our groups. There may need to be some discussion before everybody is happy. Once they are, get people to sign and date them and keep them for reference in their folders.

8.40pm-8.45pm Opening of Communion Service and Prayer of Preparation

Explain that *Exploring God* is based on the different phases of the Holy Communion service and that you are now to begin to move into the first phase which is an opening up to the work of Almighty God in your different emotions and motives.

Read the Prayer of Preparation. (If you wish, you could have copies for everybody, and will need to photocopy it, but it is very short and well known.) Allow a few moments for people to dwell on it.

Here is the version from the Church of England communion service:

Almighty God, to whom all hearts are open,
all desires known,
and from whom no secrets are hidden:
cleanse the thoughts of our hearts
by the inspiration of your Holy Spirit,
that we may perfectly love you,
and worthily magnify your holy name;
through Christ our Lord. Amen.

From *Common Worship Services and Prayers for the Church of England*, p. 168, copyright © The Archbishops' Council, 2000.

8.45pm-9.15pm Exercise on the Might of God

Now explain that you are going to do an exercise on God being mighty. You have just addressed him as Almighty God but perhaps we rarely dwell on his might in our lives and would not usually describe ourselves as experiencing his might.

Give the group members ten minutes working on their own in which to think of up to three occasions when they have experienced God as mighty. Get them to write them down. (Incidentally, don't forget that you are a group member too and need to do the exercises as conscientiously as the others.)

After this, open a time of sharing when people may share one of them (only one) with the group. Usually, after a certain opening pause people begin to share. Be prepared for the most amazing things to come out. People have shared healings, near-death experiences, dreams and visions recounted. But watch too for the less spectacular but no less mighty. A woman once testified to sensing the might of God by simply standing on the seashore, and I think we all felt the might of God in her words. There may well be a sense of awe in the room after this process. Allow the group to dwell in it a while, then round off with as few words as possible.

9.15pm-9.30pm God's Might as Creator (Isaiah 40:22-26)

Read Isaiah 40:22-26 nice and slowly. It is a great song of praise to the Creator God. It might be good to back it with music. Allow the group to let their thoughts wander during its reading and to offer their worship, each in their own hearts as they do.

It is difficult to time this exercise. You will need to judge the moment.

In any event leave enough time to explain the **Hometask** for next time, having passed round the **Hometask Sheet (Handout 1B)**. The aim of the hometask is to experience God as a Creator God and to recognise that we are made in God's image and are creative ourselves. Explain that outdoors can be anywhere. A city centre will do just as well as a country lane. Explain that they are asked to bring their response to this experience next session in some tangible form. Mere verbal recall will not do! A verbal account is fine but they must have troubled to write it down. Also other forms of permanent response are welcomed – paintings, something they found outside – whatever.

9.30pm **End**
End, as you began, promptly. Offer cups of tea or coffee, and biscuits.

Session Two: The Word of God

Outline programme

7.40pm-8pm	Arrivals.
8pm-8.20pm	Feedback on the hometask.
8.20pm-8.30pm	Reading of John 6:1-59 whilst people eat fruit and feed back.
8.30pm-9pm	Work on people's favourite menus and meals and discussion, followed by work on people's favourite spiritual food and discussion and sharing (can run on to 9.10pm).
9pm-9.15pm	Exercise on Elijah and the still small voice – 1 Kings 19:1-30.
9.15pm-9.30pm	Silence and reflection on the Scripture verses given and an outline of the hometask.

Guidance notes for leaders

Aim of Session
To help members explore a variety of ways of feeding on the Word of God, to recognise which are most attractive to them and to encourage them to broaden their repertoire.

Preparation in advance
In addition to the usual preparations for every week, you will need to prepare the following for this particular week:

- **A large plateful of different fruits**, cut up sufficiently small to be eaten with the fingers. The more exotic you can make this the better and the more the variety of fruits the better. Apples, oranges, dates, bananas, pineapple, cherries, strawberries with a few nuts as well – all are recommended. The plate needs to be of the right size to provide enough pieces of fruit for everybody. Overdo it if anything. We have found people enjoy the fruit. This plate is to stand on the central table.
- **Some other items suggestive of nourishment for the soul, to have on your central table.** The Bible, of course, but also attractive shells, small sculptures or figurines, icons, postcards of famous paintings, and small pieces of driftwood are all good ideas. The texture and colours offered by these will be nourishing in themselves.
- Some **plates and/or some paper napkins** for when it comes to eating the fruit.
- Your **Bible** ready to read from John 6:1-59 and later 1 Kings 19:1-30.
- Copies of the **Handout of Scripture verses (Handout 2A)** given as a handout during the session.
- Copies of the **Worksheet, 'My Preferences for Receiving the Word of God' (Handout 2B).**
- Copies of the **Hometask (Handout 2C)** for this session leading to the next.

7.40pm-8pm **Arrivals – with background music as usual**

8pm-8.20pm **Feedback on last session's hometask**
We allow a longish time for this. We have found this first feedback time to be particularly rewarding for all. It has often

been the time when our groups have gelled after their initial strangeness. Group members have also usually surpassed themselves in the variety and creativity of their sharing back after reflecting on their 20 minutes' worth of time outdoors. We have had woodcarvings, pottery, cookery, collages, water-colours, poetry, chalks, and mime as well as ordinary accounts in prose. Be prepared to be surprised at your group's versatility. Equally, don't worry if their offerings are fairly uniform. It is good to allow full time for these to be shared. It is good, too, to place the things shared on or around your central table for the rest of the session. It makes a lovely and powerful visual impact, indicative of the creativity gone in to them. You will need to avoid any sense of competition or comparison and to value each person's sharing for its own worth.

8.20pm-8.30pm Reading of John 6:1-59

Introduce the next activity by explaining that you are going to read this long passage. It will take about five minutes to read. Whilst you are reading the group members are free to come and take as much of the fruit as they like and eat it. Encourage them not to be bashful.

The way this usually has gone for us is that people allow a few moments before beginning to eat but then they start to take some. Incidentally, the fruit usually looks really good and they have fancied some ever since they arrived. It also has the impact of surprise when they arrive, being unusual at study groups.

By the time you have reached the later verses they will have taken all they want and be seated again. The final paragraphs contain some amazing words of Jesus. Read into that context, we have found them to have great power in themselves.

When the reading is over, allow a few moments for reflection and then take feedback.

- What was it like to listen to the Bible being read and be eating at the same time?
- How did the two forms of feeding go together?
- What struck them about the fruit when they came in? and when they were eating?
- What struck them from the passage? (Caution here – don't get into a Bible study or discussion.)

Keep the feedback very brief – just the five minutes you will have left after the reading.

8.30pm-9pm **Exercise on favourite menus and meals, followed by work on people's favourite spiritual foods (can run to 9.10pm)**
Now set people the task, in pairs, of discussing their favourite menus. What would they have for starter, main course and dessert?

When they have discussed that, they are asked to discuss together their favourite forms of spiritual food. What would correspond in spiritual terms to a starter, main course and dessert? This is always great fun and leaves people devising mouth-watering meals.

Take feedback, perhaps with people reporting back on their partner's preferences, firstly about natural foods only. Again it is great fun to hear of everybody's likes and dislikes.

Move on then to people's preferences for spiritual foods. Some will like sermons, Bible reading, tapes, books, silence, walking in the open air, poetry, music, liturgy – all in differing ways and proportions. Encourage a sense of people finding their own best ways of receiving spiritual food. Some may be released from seeking it in places not suited to them. Some others may be encouraged into new ways of deriving spiritual nourishment or to realise that they are getting such nourishment from something they had merely thought a pastime, like painting, say.

Hand out the worksheet **'My Preferences for Receiving the Word of God' (Handout 2B).** Allow people time to fill them in. Give people an opportunity to share from them. Suggest that they keep the sheet in their folder.

9pm-9.15pm **Exercise on Elijah and the still small voice – 1 Kings 19:1-13**
After this, read the above passage aloud. Ask people to react to it in general and then allow a brief discussion. See how the group members find the contrasts between the thunderstorm and the lightning and the still small voice. See if they relate to any of them. Perhaps they may have experiences of hearing God in either quiet or noisy ways. How do they try to discern when and when not 'God is in' a spiritual experience?

This exercise is no more than a dipping of a toe in the water of the vast area of listening to God. Explain this.

Express the hope that this will help them further with this elusive skill.

9.15pm-9.30pm Reflection on Scripture verses, outline the hometask

To close, hand around the **Handout (2A)** giving the **Scripture Verses**. Take at least five or six minutes in silent reflection for people to read them through. Offer them as a basis for people to use during their 10 minutes' daily silence. You might usefully then enquire with the group how their times of 10 minutes' silence are going.

Finally, explain the hometask for the coming fortnight, having handed out the **Hometask Sheet (Handout 2C)**. The aim is to increase one's awareness of the skills and value in attentive listening as a way to hearing God's voice in others and in oneself. Answer any questions. Try to make it especially clear that they are **either** basically to listen **or** be listened to by their chosen partner.

Offer suggestions on what might be included in their reflection on their listening encounter. What feelings did the time provoke? Was it an easy exercise or a sticky one? Why was this? Has it left them wanting to do more or less listening and/or talking?

Over the tea/coffee and biscuits it is fun to finish off the fruit!

Session Three: Intercession, praying for others

Outline programme

7.40pm-8pm	Arrivals.
8pm-8.15pm	Review hometask.
8.15pm-8.25pm	Walkabout, looking at the pictures. People to choose which engages them the most.
8.25pm-8.40pm	Feedback from the pictures.
8.40pm-8.50pm	Discussion on interceding, difficulties and useful methods people have.
8.50pm-9pm	Explanation of intercessory method.
9pm-9.10pm	Individual time for people to intercede.
9.10pm-9.25pm	Walkabout to get a picture from the wall, then with a prayer said aloud, place it on the table.
9.25pm-9.30pm	Explain the hometask.
9.30pm	End.

Guidance notes for leaders

Aim of Session

To explore how God is stirring within us concerns for the needs of the world and to look at improving our approach to intercessory prayer.

Preparation in advance

During the preceding weeks collect together **12 pictures from a newspaper** or topical magazine. The pictures should reflect what is going on in the world and may be of political figures, royal figures, national and international events, etc. They do not all need to be serious and could include something amusing. Before the evening begins these pictures should be bluetacked to the walls of the room where you will meet, spread randomly around the room.

Have ready copies of:

- **Intercessory method (Handout 3A).**
- **Hometask Sheet (Handout 3B).**
- **A few seeds or small bulbs** to hand to each person. We have used cress, runner bean, or crocus.
- **Central table.** As well as a candle and the bread and wine, it would be an idea to have open on the table an atlas or (if you have one) a globe, as the theme for this session is intercessions. The aim is to encourage everyone to think beyond themselves to the needs of others. You may have other suitable objects to use, e.g. a poster, praying hands figurine, a rosary, a piece of corded rope.
- **Music.**

7.40pm-8pm **Arrivals**

8pm-8.15pm **Review hometask**

The hometask for the previous session was to listen or be listened to and to reflect on that experience. Explain to the group that you now have 15 minutes in which to take feedback. As before, this is not to become a discussion, but simply time to allow folk to share what they will and for the group to receive and hold it. Explain that you are interested not in the **content** of what was said, but more in the **process** of what it was like to be listened to or to listen to someone in this way.

This may need emphasising as people rapidly get drawn into sharing content rather than reflecting on the experience. Be prepared to be surprised by the variety in the feedback. Your group will be more relaxed by now and ready to share. For some listening may be part of their daily work but they may notice a difference in the quality of the listening. We have had people who regularly listen in their job be delighted with the experience of concentrated listening to a family member. Sometimes two members of the group who did not know each other well have shared this exercise and a new friendship has resulted. For some it has proved a difficult exercise to take the plunge and talk for 20 minutes and they have experienced a whole range of emotions.

8.15pm-8.25pm Walkabout, looking at the pictures

Draw people's attention to what is round the walls of the room, as not everyone will have noticed them. Say nothing about the pictures but allow 5-10 minutes for everyone to get up, walk around the room and look at the displayed newspaper/ magazine pictures. Suggest that they think of which picture they identified with the most.

8.25pm-8.40pm Feedback from the pictures

When everyone has sat down allow about five minutes overall for each person to indicate and explain which picture engaged them most and why.

8.40pm-8.50pm Discussion on interceding, difficulties and useful methods people have

Here follows an open discussion about how people pray for others. Suggest questions like 'Do people find it easy/hard to pray for others' needs? Do they allocate time, use lists, etc.?' This aims to be a practical time with people sharing what does or does not work for them, what they have found a help or a hindrance, what difficulties they face in seeking to intercede. This can prove a very fruitful time of learning from one another.

8.50pm-9pm Explanation of intercessory method

You may wish to use the **Handout 3A** which gives a suggested method of intercessory prayer, which we have devised. It is only meant as a guide. You may want to adapt it.

9pm-9.10pm **Individual time for people to intercede**

If you still have plenty of time, allow up to 10 minutes for people to pray silently for one person using the above method.

9.10pm-9.25pm **Walkabout to get a picture from the wall, then with a prayer said aloud, place it on the table**

Encourage everyone to get up and take from the wall the news picture that most affected them. Obviously where two or more people want the same picture they will need to negotiate and compromise! Then all gather standing around the table.

Encourage everyone to say a brief prayer stimulated by the picture and then to lay the picture on the table. The prayer may be extempore or silent; whichever people are most comfortable with.

9.25pm-9.30pm **Explain the hometask**

Hand round the **Hometask (Handout 3B)**. The aim is to identify with a Bible passage by using imaging as a way of aiding intercession. It will also help prepare for the coming session by forging connections between one's inner life and Bible reading through the use of the imagination. The hometask for the next two weeks is to spend 20 minutes reading the Gospel stories of Peter's denial of Jesus (Matthew 26:69-70; Mark 14:66-68; Luke 22:55-57; and John 18:16-18, 25-27). Explain that you wish people to imagine that they are part of the scene. What can they see, hear, smell, feel? Ask them to note their reactions and to notice with whom they most identify. Where would they put themselves? The second 20 minutes is to be spent in reflection on how this exercise made them feel.

Now use the **cress seeds, runner beans, or crocus bulbs** and hand a few to each group member. These are symbols of God's life growing within us. No specific task is set, simply tell your group to do with them what they will, but to be sure to spend time thinking about them in the next few weeks. This simple act has been very positive for at least one member of each of our groups. We have had hilarious sessions comparing the growth of runner bean seeds. Each seed may be a parable of dormant life awaiting awakening, and growing a few cress seeds often recalls childhood memories. If there is time, check out how the daily 10 minutes' silent prayer is going.

9.30pm **End**

Coffee/tea.

Session Four: 'I believe'

Outline programme

8pm-8.15pm	Report back on previous week's homework.
8.15pm-8.45pm	Exercise on what has strengthened and weakened our faith over the last 10 years.
8.45pm-9.15pm	Bible study: Matthew 11:2-6 and Luke 7:18-23.
9.15pm-9.25pm	Firelight. Time to bathe in the undergirding arms of Jesus' faith in us. Reading of 2 Timothy 1:12 – 'I know whom I have believed'. Possibly play extracts from the *Messiah*. Candles lit. End by saying together the Nicene Creed or by singing 'We believe'.
9.25pm-9.30pm	Explain hometask and round off.

Guidance notes for leaders

Aim of Session
To explore the realm of faith and doubt within each group member and how to work with this to deepen our relationship and journey into God.

Preparation in advance
- Set the centre table with a **bowl of floating flower blooms and a floating candle.**
- Have a **Bible** open at 2 Timothy 1:8-12.
- Have ready copies of **the Concentric Circles (Handout 4A) and of the Hometask (Handout 4B)** for everyone.
- Have ready copies of the **Nicene Creed**, or alternatively some music to which the group may sing a setting of the Creed such as **'We believe'** by Graham Kendrick.

7.40pm-8pm **Arrivals**

8pm-8.15pm **Report back on previous week's hometask**
Last session's hometask was to read and reflect on the scripture passages detailing Peter's denial of Jesus. Allow time for people to share their reflections, how they felt reading the passages and whom they identified with. Give an opportunity for folk to share anything they have written or prepared. Again people are to be encouraged to share only if they wish. We have found people readily identified with the different characters in the story, including the cockerel! You may find people a little reticent so have ready some open questions such as 'Who did you identify with? How easy was it to imagine you were there?'

Similarly people may share something about the seed/bulb they received. What had people done with it? Was there any growth already? You may wish to refer to the seed at each subsequent meeting. We have found that it builds up a sense of fun and playfulness, whilst at the same time continuing to symbolise the growth of our engagement with God within us. Allow 15 minutes for this exercise.

8.15pm-8.45pm **Exercise on what has strengthened and weakened our faith during our life**
Introduce the theme taken from the opening words of the

creed 'I believe in God'. Explain that for this exercise the group will be given 10 minutes silence to think and jot down anything that they feel has really strengthened their faith in God or weakened their faith during their life. It may be something big or small, but it will have significance for them. Remember the group leader needs to take part in this exercise too! Then allow a good time for people to share with the group and respond to this. We have always found this to be an extremely valuable exercise. Often one is humbled and challenged by people's contributions. Some have remarkable stories to share. Often the contributions are inspiring or heart-breaking. Some group members are relieved to recognise that they are not alone in facing doubt, or to know that others have had similar difficult experiences. For some it will be the first time that they have openly shared a deep grief and there is enormous power in the group to hold them in their listening and not to condemn. Others will have had an unshakeable faith, or moments of revelation they wish to share. This time needs sensitive handling, particularly as to rounding off and moving on to the next stage.

8.45pm-9.15pm Bible study Matthew 11:2-6 and Luke 7:18-23

Read together the two passages out loud and then give a moment or two for people to reflect on them. Ask for comments and have ready some prompting questions such as 'Why did John send his disciples to Jesus? What do you think was going on in his mind? Why did Jesus answer in that way? What does this make you think?' Perhaps one of the many things that these passages shed light on is that even great biblical figures like John the Baptist had times of doubt and uncertainty, and Jesus understands that. Ask the group if they relate to John in his doubts at all. Ask if they feel times of doubt for them have ever grown through to become times of revelation or of a deeper certainty of faith. Often, we find, group members have shied away from their experiences of doubt through shame. Encourage them to regard doubt as a seedbed for enhanced belief.

9.15pm-9.25pm Firelight and/or candlelight

There is now time to reflect meditatively on Jesus' faith in us and his faithfulness. In winter it would be appropriate, if you can, to create a mellow glow with firelight. We have been able to have a log fire but this will vary from setting to setting. In summer try to create a tranquil atmosphere, possibly using floating candles and flower heads. Whatever the season, it is good to have several candles around the room and to turn off the electric lighting. Ask everyone to relax and close their eyes and then read very slowly the Bible verses from 2 Timothy 1:8-12. Read it again and then play quietly any music extracts you have chosen for this time. End by reading just verse 12 alone from the passage and then by saying together the Nicene Creed or by singing 'We believe'.

9.25pm-9.30pm Explain Hometask and round off

This session's task is to explore the world of our relationships in preparation for the next session. Give out the **Concentric Circles (Handout 4A) and Hometask (Handout 4B)**. Note that group members need **two** copies each. Explain the task carefully to the group. It is quite a personal and stretching exercise they are being asked to do. Stress that, as it says on the handout, there will be **no feedback on the content of this task.** What they write will remain their private property. There will be a brief opportunity to share how *doing the exercise* felt, but nothing on the content of what they have written.

9.30pm End

Coffee/tea and biscuits as ever at the end.

Session Five: Our sins and forgiveness

Outline programme

7.40pm-8pm	Arrivals.
8pm-8.15pm	Recap on homework.
8.15pm-8.30pm	Work individually on listing those we need to forgive.
8.30pm-9pm	Open time to share feelings/discuss how and what you do to forgive others.
9pm-9.10pm	Worktime on our attitude. Meditation on the self-offering of Jesus (pictures).
9.10pm-9.25pm	Symbolic tearing/offering of our willingness to forgive. Breaking of bread/pouring of wine.
9.25pm-9.30pm	Hometask and close.

Guidance notes for leaders

Aims of Session
Group members have looked at the pattern of their relationships as their hometask in preparation for this session. Its aim is now to explore the realm of forgiveness in their relationships. This includes their relationship with God as well as with others.

Preparation in advance
For Session Five you will need:

- Enough copies of the **'I Forgive You' sheet (Handout 5A)**.
- Possibly, the **facility to burn** half of people's 'I Forgive You' handout.
- For the **central table**: as well as the usual bread and wine and any other ever-present things you have opted for, have items which touch on the issue of forgiveness. We have used small posters and postcards of paintings depicting the crucifixion or symbols of it. We have added to the table for this session some extra crosses in addition to our regular one. There are an abundance of small wooden crosses in different styles around. Your local Christian bookshop will have a variety. Do not forget the power of abstract things to evoke a subject like forgiveness as well. A piece of pottery or a dried flower, even something broken, could be very effective. As ever – feel free to use your imagination.
- Your **Bible** and enough Bibles for all, ready for a short Bible study on Jesus at the House of Simon the Pharisee (Matthew 26:6-13; Mark 14:3-9; John 12:1-8).
- Enough copies of the **Hometask (Handout 5B)**.

7.40pm-8pm **Arrivals**

8pm-8.15pm **Recap on Hometask**
You promised last time that there would be no sharing from people's homework, because it was so personal and searching. Honour this, even if your group has been a very open one in sharing times up to this point.

But it has been valuable in our groups on the whole to allow time for people to say how the exercise felt for them, without them betraying anything of its content. You will recall the work was to do with the two sets of concentric circles and the peopling of their lives.

Was it painful or joyful for them? Easy or hard? A new way of thinking or not?

8.15pm-8.30pm **Work individually on listing those we need to forgive**

When the review of feelings about the hometask is done, next give out the **'I Forgive You' Handout (Handout 5A)**. Let people look at them for a moment. Then set the exercise of listing on the left-hand side of their sheet the people they need to forgive. Allow the 15 minutes. We have found this one of more unpredictable exercises we do. With one big group nobody (except us!) felt they had any need to forgive anybody else. In a very small group there was a group member who felt the main benefit of the whole course was to be enabled, through this exercise, to forgive someone over a long-standing and bitter dispute. You may need also to explain that people can include any issues they have over forgiving God.

8.30pm-9pm **Open time to share feelings/discuss how and what you do to forgive others**

As we have just said, it is difficult to predict what will be your group members' reaction to this exercise. It may seem like a non-issue to them. If so, dig a little deeper with them. Ask questions like:

- Has anybody wounded them?
- What do they do when someone offends them?
- Do they unfailingly turn the other cheek?

You may discover that some of them are evading their real feelings somewhat. Others may despair of ever forgiving. Certainly forgiveness for long-standing hurts can be a life-long job. We had a group member who had a history of abuse in their childhood. Forgiveness for them was a big matter. With people who show such large forgiveness issues, avoid the temptation to try and solve their problems in the session. You won't. Also avoid discussion on the content of people's forgiveness lists. Work on getting people to share what they find practically helpful when it comes to forgiveness. People often have private methods that it may be good to learn from. These range from little tips like counting to 10, through to writing a letter to Jesus about the offence, or confronting the person concerned, or blessing and praying for the person and so on. We have had some fruitful discussions along these lines.

Have up your sleeve, as it were, **a brief Bible study** on the story of the woman who anoints Jesus' feet at the house of Simon the Pharisee (Matthew 26:6-13; Mark 14:3-9, John 12:1-8). It is full of issues to do with forgiveness. You may feel your group discussion would benefit from being focused on a Bible passage. You may even wish to start this section of the evening by looking at it first. Some questions to ask the group about the reading would be 'Who do you identify with and why? How does this passage make you feel? Why do you think Jesus responds as he does? Do we have anything to learn today?'

9pm-9.10pm **Work time on our attitude**

Meditation of the offering of Jesus

The aim of this meditation time is to explore God's offer of forgiveness to us all through the sacrifice of Jesus. Offer your special aids to forgiveness on the central table for people's use as they work and write. Encourage them to come to the table and take things back to their places if they wish – the pictures of the passion, paintings found in art books, or postcards obtained from art galleries, the crosses, the other, perhaps abstract, things you have used. Give people time to look and meditate, play appropriate background music and then move people on to do work on the right-hand side of the **'I Forgive You'** sheets. Ask them to look at each person named on the left-hand side and then write in on the right-hand side their new attitude. Give them permission to be real about this. They may be only able to make a shift of attitude in one or two cases. They may not be able to offer full and free forgiveness yet. Stress that forgiveness for most of us is many-layered. Explain that if we are doing our conscious best to forgive as much as we are able, then that is a start and it is acceptable to God.

9.10pm-9.25pm Symbolic tearing/offering of our willingness to forgive
Breaking of bread/pouring of wine

When people are ready, get them to tear their sheets in half. Then ask them to fold or screw up the left-hand side and place it wherever you have decided to have them. This could be:

- In the fire.
- In a basin where you will then burn them.
- On the table before the cross or the bread and wine.
- Screwed up in a bowl from which you will throw them away.

Next, as the final act of the session, break the bread and pour some wine from a jug into your chalice or glass. The idea of this is twofold. Firstly, it is meant to give your group members hope and inspiration in their walk of forgiveness. Jesus' body and blood are the ultimate in forgiveness. He has been there before us, he will be with us in our endeavours to forgive, and he has plumbed the depths of forgiveness.

Secondly, it is meant to convey to the group that an auspicious time in the group's life is upon them. After all the weeks of work they will, next session, reach the climax of all their endeavours and share in a final celebration of the Eucharist. Pouring out the elements aims to leave them with a sense of anticipation.

We want to stress that this act is not formally sacramental. It is not formally part of a celebration of the Eucharist. It is purely an educational symbol for the group.

9.25pm-9.30pm Hometask

Hand round the **Hometask** sheet they will be asked to do. (**Handout 5B**) The hometask is to spend 20 minutes reading through the five sessions that have been completed. Explain that, now the course is nearing its end, there is enormous value in looking back and reviewing what they have thought and felt and learned in the preceding weeks on the course. The aim of this hometask is to reflect back and then look beyond the end of the course. With this in mind, the second 20 minutes are to be spent in thinking and writing a simple resolution.

'After the end of this course I am going to keep on/start/stop doing ....'

Coffee, tea and biscuits to follow as usual.

Session Six: Celebration

Outline programme

7.40pm-8pm	Arrivals.
8pm-8.20pm	Recap on hometask and work on reviewing course using the *Review Form* (**Handout 6A**).
8.20pm-8.40pm	Mutual appreciation exercise, people giving each other words of appreciation.
8.40pm-8.50pm	Holy Communion – celebrated and distributed.
8.50pm-9.10pm	Ministry to each other.
9.10pm-9.25pm	Songs.
9.25pm-9.30pm	Close.

Guidance notes for leaders

Aims of Session

The aim of this final session is to bring together a sense of all that has been achieved so far and then to celebrate it in a final act of fellowship at the Lord's Supper.

Preparation in advance

For this, the final session, you will need:

- To have arranged to **celebrate the Holy Communion** with your group. What this requires will differ very much from group to group. You may need to involve a **visiting minister**. You may need to prepare an **order of service**. You will need to provide **bread and wine** in forms acceptable to your group. You will need to give thoughtful preparation to the layout of your **central table** and what **communion vessels** you are going to use. Taken as a whole though, we recommend as simple a form of communion as fits with your group's tradition.
- Enough copies of the **Review Form (Handout 6A)**.
- Assuming you are going to sing, enough copies of the **words to the final song or songs** you have chosen, and the means to sing them! By this we mean a backing tape or an arrangement with any musical members of the group to play or lead the singing.
- Have ready a **Blessing** of some sort to end both the session and the whole course. We recommend ***Irish Blessings*** **(Running Press, Philadelphia, USA, 1999)** but you will readily find others.
- If you are opting to do this, enough **parting gifts** to send each member away with. (Suggestions would be a prayercard, a bookmark, or a picture postcard of an explorer.)
- Something celebratory as the **refreshments**. (Ideas for this are given in the guidelines dealing with the end of the final meeting below.)

7.40pm-8pm **Arrivals**

8pm-8.20pm **Work on reviewing course using the Review Form**

The hometask should have helped people to reflect on the course. Rather than take feedback at this point, hand round the course **Review Form (Handout 6A)** and ask them to fill them in. You may prefer to do something else with this time and give the review forms out as they leave, hoping to receive them back later. Be warned though! Bitter experience both of our own negligence in chasing them up and in our former group members' in sending them on has taught us that the great majority never come back – and they are an invaluable resource for you.

The other advantage about filling them in during this final session is that it continues the habit of reflection for your group, begun in last session's hometask.

Assure your group that the form is anonymous and that anyway only you will read it. Explain that filling it in will help you in the leadership of future groups. If they wish to keep their original, arrange to have a copy made.

You will see that the form uses visual responses as well as purely verbal, and it tries to cover the different aspects of the course.

Make sure you fill one in yourself fully and sincerely. This is only good practice. It will allow you to realise your own experience of the group. You may wish to stop the writing with five minutes or so to spare. In this time you could take some verbal feedback. If you do we suggest you ask people to speak of what stands out the most for them on the course so far. This need not be a good thing, though on the whole it will be.

8.20pm-8.40pm Mutual appreciation exercise, people giving each other words of appreciation

This is perhaps the nicest but most delicate bit of the whole course. How you do it will depend on the size of your group. We find if you are six or less you can focus on each person in turn and ask everybody else to say what they have most appreciated about that individual's contribution to the group's life. If you are seven or more you will need to alter the method for reasons of time. We usually go round our circle in one direction with everyone voicing their appreciation of the person on their right. And then go round the other way with everybody repeating this for the person on their left.

You can imagine the slight intake of breath that accompanies the announcement of this exercise! But press on. We have always found that by this last session groups are sufficiently secure with each other to do this without embarrassment or hurt. In fact, far from being hurtful, this exercise is profoundly upbuilding. Mostly, people are astounded to hear the good they have done to others simply by being group members with them. Most of us go around with appalling self-images and it is deeply good to hear positive truths spoken about ourselves, which are sincerely meant. We have both been part of his exercise plenty of times now and it has never failed to surprise us with its loveliness.

8.40pm-8.50pm Holy Communion – celebrated and distributed

Now is the moment to celebrate the Communion. We only allow 10 minutes in our schedule. We recommend a brief act of celebration with the minimum of ritual and liturgy. But, no harm if you and your group want it longer. If you are having a visiting minister, and they offer you any flexibility, we recommend you keep it as simple as possible.

We recommend the group stands in a circle to celebrate the communion and passes the elements from member to member, but again, this may need to differ for your group.

8.50pm-9.10pm Prayer for and prophesy to each other (optional)

It can be very effective to take some time to pray for one another at this point, although we have omitted this prayer slot many more times than we have included it, depending on the time taken to celebrate the communion.

If you do decide to include it, it is good practice to ask people to identify ***one*** main request for prayer. How you then pray for one another will depend on people's familiar practice of prayer. Some groups may be able to practise extempore mutual prayer. Others may feel happier with a time of silent prayer. Or you may need to do the praying. You may need to balance the praying in some way such that you ask people to pray for one other person in the group. You may even like to pass some object around the circle as the praying is going on as a sign of the circle of prayer moving round.

You may wish to add prophetic prayer to this time. There is no doubt that words of prophecy spoken over people can be very memorable. But beware of time – prophecy tends to take time in our experience and beware of overload – people have already heard and given some very personal material in the appreciation session. That may be sufficient for one night.

9.10pm-9.25pm Songs

As we said in 'Planning and Preparation' we do recommend the inclusion of a time of singing. This is so even if you have not used singing in the course so far, but it is up to you, as is what to sing. You can ask for suggestions from the group, or, failing that, you will know your group well enough to be able to chose something appropriate and to their liking.

When you have sung (and this is the occasion when, if your group seems to want to overrun a little, we suggest you let them), then end with a chosen **Blessing**. Either say it yourselves or ask the minister to say it or all say it together to each other. It can be good to save the **Peace** from the communion service until now and have that as your last formal act. Our groups finish with everybody going around hugging everybody else, but you do not have to be that touchy-feely.

9.25pm-9.30pm Close

Coffee to end.

As well as the usual coffee and tea, try to mark the end of the group's life with something special by way of refreshments. Mostly, we have found the season of the year comes in to play here. You may have run up to Christmas or Easter with your meetings so you can go for mince pies or simnel cake and stuff like that. If it is midsummer, try strawberries and cream. We have had a number of unexpected offerings brought by group members at this point, including some marvellous 'icky-dicks' which taste as good as they sound disgusting. You may like to get your group members all to bring along a sweet or savouries, and make a party of it. If you have decided to use them, hand round the **parting gifts**.

Debriefing Afterwards

After a journey of exploration is over it is important to debrief. Much vital information is to be gained by this, which will make any future explorations more fruitful. This can range from practical matters, which could be improved upon another time, to deeper lessons to do with inner attitudes and outlooks.

It is the same with the *Exploring God* course. It is good to reflect on it once it is over. This is true both for group leaders and members. Here, lessons can be learned which also can range from quite simple practical things to profound shifts in spiritual outlook.

In this final chapter we offer some suggestions as to how this might be done. We begin with ourselves as group leaders and then move on to group members.

A debriefing for group leaders

We suggest that somewhere between a month and fortnight after your course has ended you hold **a debriefing meeting** as leaders. Even if you have been the sole leader still hold the meeting! Allow a couple of hours for this, aiming to do it steadily and thoroughly.

We suggest you use the **Debrief Sheet** we supply (**Handout 7A**) but it is up to you. You will in any event want to cover the general areas mentioned in it. Where it comes to evaluating your skills as leaders, always emphasise the positives and only bring up one negative area per person at once.

And don't forget to include your own evaluation of the course as group members yourselves.

Here are a few points worth remembering as you use the Sheet:

- It is good to begin with some general overall impressions and to work through as wide a range of impressions as possible, hence the questions in **section one of the Sheet**. Where you are a team of leaders it is well worth some evaluation of your mutual strengths and weaknesses. A good technique for this is for the other leaders to list all the good qualities someone has shown and then pick just one thing (and only one) that might bear some improvement. We don't put this on the sheet but it is worth doing.

- You will notice, in **Group Life (section two)**, that we have included some non-verbal exercises of evaluation. This is designed to assist you to think intuitively about how your group has gone.
- Work steadily through the detail in **Sections Three and Four of the Sheet.** Most groups, we find, go very well on the whole. It is tempting in the sense of overall well-being to gloss over areas of detail, which you 'got away with' when delivering the course, but which could be improved upon. This is hard work but has led to our revising our *Exploring God* courses quite extensively.
- This leads to the next thing. Don't be afraid to adapt what you have done even if it works away from the course as we have presented it to you. It is not set in stone. The whole idea of exploration is the discovery of new things. God is limitless. You may very well have discovered new areas of helping people explore their God, which you should keep in your future work and which differs from our approach. If so – good! Well done! Scrap our material and move on into your own.
- If you find, after using the Debrief Sheet, that you are motivated to plan another course, it is good to get on with it, even if the start of the next course is some way away. On the other hand try not to assume you will automatically do another course. Try to assess the merits and demerits of doing another one each time.

Following up the course for group members

In addition to the value of your own debrief as leaders there is the vital last task of helping your group members retain and build on the good they have received in the group. We suggest the following steps as the best ways to do this.

- Firstly, soon after the end of the course, send them a nice letter enclosing their '**How to keep on exploring' Sheet. (Handout 7B)**. Don't fall into the temptation of giving them this at your final group session. You might like to tell them then that they can expect it to come, but send it separately. In the letter, thank them very much for their contribution to the group. You may like to add in, for each, a personal note of appreciation for what they themselves especially brought to the group. Explain that you are now enclosing the promised **'How to keep on exploring' Sheet** for their use. It works through the main areas of discovery the course is designed to open up. It is self-explanatory. Say you hope that it will be of help as they try now to keep on exploring God for themselves. Suggest that they do not try and do everything on the Sheet all at once, for fear of overload. Perhaps rather they might look for the two or three things that they have most enthusiasm for. But say, too, if they have bigger ambitions that that, you would not wish to get in their way! Close by giving the time, date and venue of your **Follow-Up Meeting** and inviting them along. Say you will be having a central table at this meeting as ever before and if anyone wants to help you with it, they have only to ask.

- Secondly, **hold a Follow-up Meeting**. Time this at about one month to six weeks after the end of the course. As far as you can, hold it at the same venue and time as your group sessions were held. Still do the 20-minute quiet time for arrivals as in the course proper. Also, still have a central table and liase beforehand with any group member who has asked to help with it. The design we leave to you. You will, by now, be seasoned table setters, we trust!
- We also leave to you the particular way you wish to approach the follow up meeting. On the whole we think it a more engaging dynamic to let group members speak about their hopes and plans to keep exploring God as they wish and from their own starting points, rather than to work systematically down the Sheet. But it is up to you. Certainly if some area given on the Sheet has not been picked up by any group members, then it is worth looking at it briefly as well. If there seems to be some collective reason why it has been avoided, it is worth probing a little to find it out. This may even prove to be the most important area for your group to try and work on in the future, precisely because they are all avoiding it. But this is not too likely a scenario.

- We do suggest you leave a good time at the end of your meeting for mutual prayer and encouragement. How you organise this will depend on your group's understanding and experience of prayer, something you will well know by now. Some groups will move relaxedly in the realms of extempore prayer for each other and in prophecy. If so well and good. But don't try and force this if it is not familiar to them. Silent prayer is good, of course. Again you could delegate that each group member prays in any way they feel able for one of their fellow group members. This can evoke some lovely humble, even stumbling prayers yet of great power.
- End the meeting with the **Blessing** you have chosen.
- How much you follow up your group members beyond this is will depend upon a number of factors such as the nature of any normal pastoral charges you have over them, who else is pastorally responsible for them, just how much care you can realistically maintain and so on. The bottom line is that your basic responsibility to them was to deliver the course caringly and well. Once you have done that you need to feel free to let the good they have received work on. The best thing may be for your group members to move on without you.

Exploring God

Photocopiable Handouts for Course Members

1A Exploring God

Contract

In coming on the *Exploring God* course I am happy to contract myself to the following things:

1. To attend every session of the course, unless it is absolutely impossible, and if I need to miss a session to send an apology in advance.

2. To be punctual and in my place ready for the course start by 8pm at the latest. I understand that the room will be prepared and available for me from 7.40pm onwards should I wish to use it.

3. To treat as confidential personal material shared with the group by course members.

4. Conscientiously to undertake the home tasks set between sessions. I understand that this will be a time commitment of 40 minutes, taken either in one session or in two 20-minute sessions.

5. To regard the support materials provided on the course as important aids to the course, to read them and respect them.

6. To undertake to spend 10 minutes per day in stillness and silence. I understand that this can be either in one 10 minute sitting or in two 5 minutes. I will treat myself gently in this task and forgive myself when I find I have failed it.

Signed..

Date...

1B Exploring God

Task to be completed by Week Two

Please would you between now and the next session:

1. Spend **at least 20 minutes** in one continuous session outdoors somewhere. This may be your garden, a park, the street, the middle of London, on a boat, literally anywhere, so long as it is outdoors. During this time, would you please try to use all your five senses, taste, touch, smell, sight and hearing, to imbibe the experience as fully as you can, though without striving.

2. Would you please then, either immediately following or at some later time before the next *Exploring God* session, take a further period of 20 minutes in one continuous session to reflect on your experience of being outdoors. The form your reflection takes needs please to be a permanent form which you can then bring to the next session for sharing. It could be a piece of writing, a computer graphic, a piece of drawing, or a piece of modelling. It could be a symbol, something perhaps you discovered when you were outdoors and were able to bring with you. It could be a posture of your body.

2A Exploring God

Session Two: The Word of God

Psalm 81:10

I am the Lord your God,
who brought you up out of Egypt.
Open wide your mouth and I will fill it.

Psalm 119:103

How sweet are your words to my taste,
sweeter than honey to my mouth!

Psalm 34:8

Taste and see that the Lord is good;
blessed is the man who takes refuge in him.

John 6:35

Then Jesus declared, 'I am the bread of life. He who comes to me will never go hungry, and he who believes in me will never be thirsty.'

John 6:55

'For my flesh is real food and my blood is real drink.'

2B Exploring God

Session Two: The Word of God

Worksheet 1

My preferences for receiving the Word of God:

A. My three strongest preferences for receiving the Word of God are:

1. ....

2. ....

3. ....

B. (If applicable) I would do better, for now, to avoid trying to receive the Word of God by:

....

....

Name: ....

2C Exploring God

Session Two: The Word of God

Hometask Sheet

Task to be completed by Week Three

During the next fortnight would you please:

1. Find a willing partner and *either* talk to them for 20 minutes unbroken, although they are allowed to ask prompting questions but it mustn't become a discussion. Basically, you must be talking and them listening. *Or* do it in reverse, they talk and you listen.

2. Reflect on the experience of being listened to, or of listening, and come ready next time with some reflections to share with the group.

Also, don't forget the commitment to spend 10 minutes a day in silence and, if possible, reflect on that experience a bit as well.

3A Exploring God

Session Three: A suggested method for intercession

1. **Releasing**
   We release the people we are going to intercede for to God. We try to acknowledge, and then drop, all our preconceptions about them and all our hidden agendas for them.

2. **Confession and forgiveness**
   We confess to God and ask forgiveness for all our sinful attitudes toward the person or people we are going to pray for. Then we also forgive them anything and everything we may feel they have done against us.

3. **Stillness and listening to God**
   Before praying anything for these people we try to attune ourselves to God's best will for them by stilling our own souls and trying to listen for his Spirit's lead in what to pray for.

4. **Intercession**
   If we get such a lead, which can often be remarkably creative ideas, begin to pray about it. Ideas often flow then in a way which they wouldn't have done without using the method so far. If no lead seems to come, we are content to remain still and silent, simply holding the people and their needs up to God without words.

5. **Action**
   Often when we intercede for people it leads to action. There may be an encouraging word to pass on. There may be a need of reconciliation with them. There may be some good we can do toward them. There may be a letter to write, a cheque to send, or some other form of action. It is important to regard this action as part of the praying and not separate.

6. **Recording**
   It's really good to keep a written record of our intercessions by way of a journal or log, and to record answers to our prayers when they occur.

3B Exploring God

Session Three: 'Believing'

Hometask

1. **Please would you read Peter's denial of Jesus (Matthew 26:69-70; Mark 14:66-68; Luke 22:55-57, and John 18:16-18, 25-27).**

   Then, for 20 minutes, imagine being present at the scene. Describe or draw it (use symbols if you wish). Note your reactions. Who do you identify with and where would you put yourself?

   Then, for a second 20 minutes, reflect on how you feel. What emotions are evoked within you by imagining being present at the scene

2. Please accept these seeds from us and do with them what you will. Take time to reflect about them in the remaining weeks.

4A Exploring God

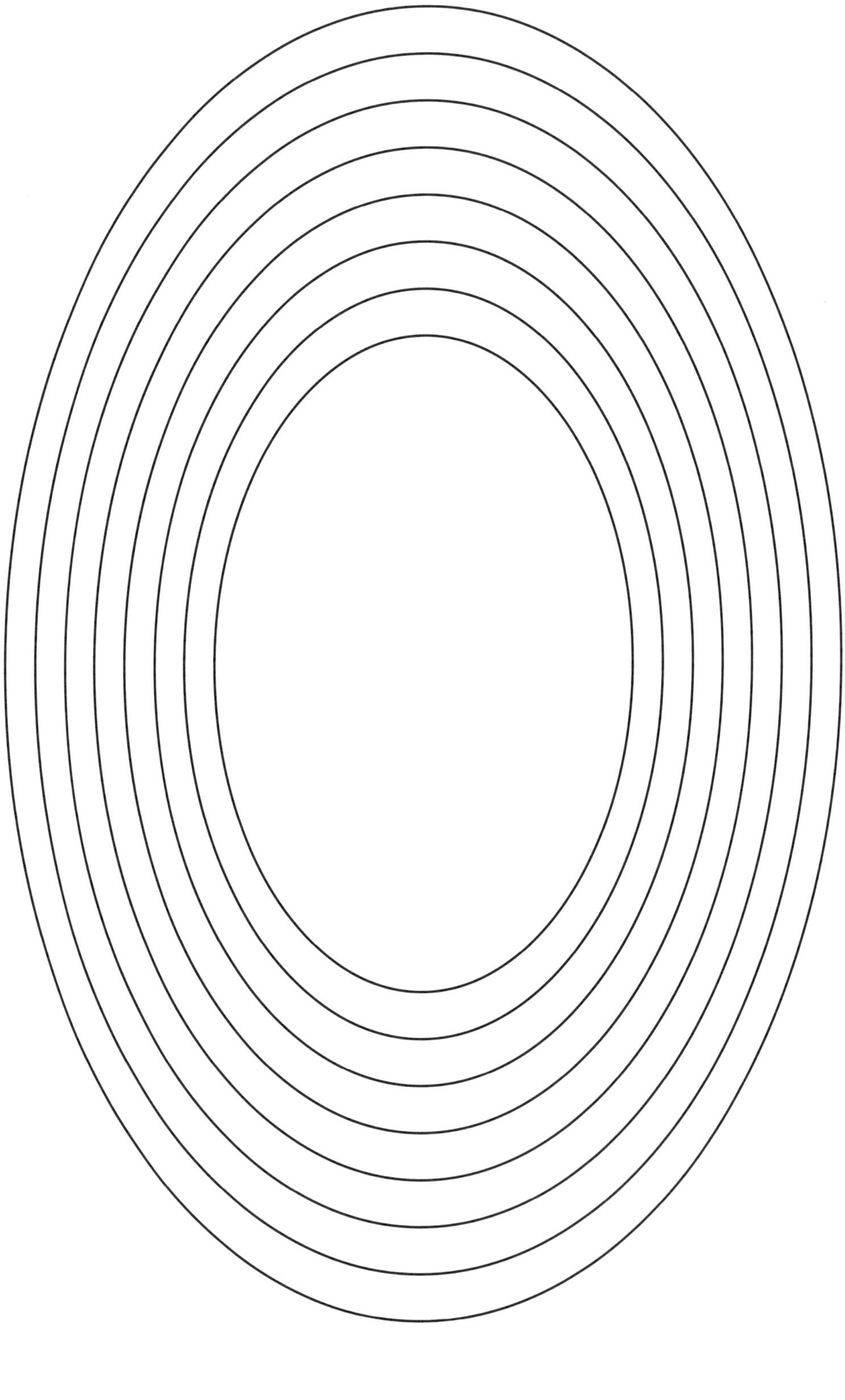

4B Exploring God

Session Four

Hometask

A. For **20 minutes** would you please:

1. Plot the people in your life on this diagram of concentric ovals. Imagine yourself at the centre and draw or write in the names of those with whom you share your life, in the place on the diagram that seems most appropriate to you.

2. Once you have done this reflect for a little while on your reactions to the diagram as you now have it. Ask yourself these questions:

   Do I like how it looks?

   Do I feel I have enough space?

   Do I feel isolated?

   Are there enough people in my life?

   Are the people in a balanced position for me?

   Are there people missing I would like to include?

   Are there people there I would like to not have in my diagram?

   What do I feel about the people there?

   Are there people I met in the pictures around the walls I want to bring into my diagram?

   What do I think God feels about the shape and content of my diagram?

   Do I want to take any decisions about the peopling of my life?

B. For another 20 minutes take the second diagram and draw on it the people and patterns of relating you would regard as ideal. Compare it with the first one. How different is it? Think about the similarities. Dwell on them. Give thanks for them. Think about the differences. What do they make you feel? What do you want to do about them? What do you feel you can do about them? What do you feel God wants you to feel and think and do about your pattern of relationships?

People I need to forgive

My new attitude

5B Exploring God

Hometask

Week One

The hometask is to spend 20 minutes thinking back over the five sessions that have been completed. There is enormous value in looking back and reviewing what you have thought and felt and learned in the preceding weeks on the course. The aim of this hometask is to reflect back and then look beyond the end of the course.

Week Two

With this in mind, the second 20 minutes are to be spent in thinking and writing a simple resolution.

'After the end of this course
I am going to keep on/start/stop doing

....'

NB There will be no showing of this homework. It is personal to you.

6A Exploring God

Review Form

Please would you be so kind as to fill in this form, partly for your own sake to help you review the value of being on this course, and partly for our benefit to help us as we assess our delivery of it in the future.

1. What stands out to you as the best thing about the course for you? Please describe it briefly and the reason why it blessed you in that way.......................................

   ....

   ....

2. What has been the worst thing about the course for you? Please answer in the same way as the previous question.

   ....

   ....

   ....

3. Please make a list of the overall benefits to you of being on the course. ....

   ....

   ....

4. What feelings do these benefits stir in you? ....

....

....

5. What have been the most difficult or uncomfortable parts of being on the course for you? ....

....

....

6. What feelings have these difficulties stirred in you? ....

....

....

7. What key words or phrases sum up your experience of being on the course? ....

....

....

8. If you have to describe being on the course in one word, what would it be? Please write it in this box. If you wish to draw or decorate your word in any way, or use graphics in any way to amplify it, please use the space provided.

9. Please write a thought giving your overall reaction to the following things we tried to provide:

   Space for reflection

   Novelty

   Creativity

   Exploring God

   Honesty

   Friendship

   Variety

   Self-expression

   Food and drink

10. Any further advice or suggestions to us?

Thank you very much for being on *Exploring God.* We do hope you found it beneficial overall, and have been grateful to share it with you.

7A Exploring God

Debrief Sheet for Leaders

1. **Generally for you as leaders**
   - Are you glad you led the course? ....
   - What was the most satisfying thing as a leader? ....

     ....
   - What was the most difficult thing as a leader? ....

     ....

     ....
   - Write an answer to 'The thing I have learnt most from leading *Exploring God* is' ....

     ....

     ....

2. **Group Life**

   General comments on the group ....

   ....

   ....

   If the group was an animal, what would it be? (draw it)

   If the group was a shape, what would it be? (draw it)

If the group was a colour, what would it be?

Discuss together what your reactions teach you about the group.

3. **Preparations**

Mark out of 10 and comment on:

Whole course planning $\frac{}{10}$ ....

Venue $\frac{}{10}$ ....

Timing and timekeeping $\frac{}{10}$ ....

Liaison with minister $\frac{}{10}$ ....

Publicity $\frac{}{10}$ ....

Resources $\frac{}{10}$ ....

Seating $\frac{}{10}$ ....

Central table $\frac{}{10}$ ....

Music $\frac{}{10}$ ....

If we did it again we would change ....

....

4. **Each session**

Think back over each session.

Session 1 – Almighty God

The best thing was ....

....

The worst thing was ....

....

Lessons to learn ....

....

Session 2 – The Word of God

The best thing was ....

....

The worst thing was ....

....

Lessons to learn ....

....

Session 3 – Intercession, praying for others

The best thing was ....

....

The worst thing was ....

....

Lessons to learn ....

....

Session 4 – 'I believe'

The best thing was ....

....

The worst thing was ....

....

Lessons to learn ....

....

Session 5 – Our sins and forgiveness

The best thing was ....

....

The worst thing was...

....

Lessons to learn ....

....

Session 6 – Celebration

The best thing was ....

....

The worst thing was...

....

Lessons to learn ....

....

5. **Plans for future**

Would you plan to run another course?.....................................

If no, why? ....

....

If yes, why? ....

....

If yes, what action will you take?
(Times, dates, publicity, leadership, etc.) ....

....

....

....

7B Exploring God

How to keep on exploring

Guide to Course Members

We hope you have enjoyed being on the *Exploring God* course. Indeed we hope it has been more than enjoyment, but a profound experience between you and your God. Most people who have done *Exploring God* leave the course wanting to try and carry on doing at least some of the things they were doing whilst the course was happening. This guide gives you some suggestions of different areas of exploration you might like to keep on with. It is probably best not to try them all, but here they are.

(a) **Celebration**

In our final session, as well as celebrating the Holy Communion, we celebrated each other. It is important to keep on knowing our worth in the love of God and the fellowship of other believers. You might want to think about how to keep on being able to be appreciated and appreciate others, and to celebrate God in the bread and the wine. Do you recall what was said about you? Have you written it down?

In order to keep on celebrating and being celebrated I am going to

....

....

(b) **A daily time of silence** (10 minutes or so)

You will remember this was built into the course. You might like to think over whether you found it beneficial or not and whether you can continue with it or not, or even try it more than once a day. Think it over and then fill in the statement below.

I intend to keep on having a daily time of silence Yes/No

It will last for .... minutes.

I will try it at .... (time of day)

I will try more times in the day Yes/No

My other times will be ....

(c) **An actual physical focus of prayer**

You will remember that on the course we had our central table as the focus of all our group sessions. You might like to try to create a similar thing for yourself in one way or another. Here is a list of possibilities, ranging from small-scale to large.

- **Carrying something with you** all the time as an aid to prayer, such as a cross or a prayer rope or a prayer card or a small icon.
- **Putting something on a sideboard or small table somewhere** in your house that will be a focus for prayer. Again, ideas would be a small cross or icon, even an ornament or piece of driftwood, or something else similar to what you saw used as part of *Exploring God.*
- **A prayer place**, e.g. a particular chair you sit in to help you focus and pray, perhaps near to a small table.
- **A prayer table.** If you are able to do it in your home, create a prayer table similar to the one used on the course and have it somewhere permanently and maybe sit close to it for your times of silence.
- **A whole room for prayer.** If you are lucky enough to be able to do this, it is a wonderful thing to have a room in your house that is only used for prayer. You are able then to perhaps have a particular comfortable chair or prayer stool or cushion, a prayer table, the room decorated in a way that you find helpful to prayer, and put things on the walls, maps for prayer for the world, or posters and so on.

(d) **Giving yourself permission to be creative**

You might remember some of the wonderful things people did when we made you take time to be creative. Perhaps you want to retain that in your life somehow. Think about it and answer for yourself the question below.

I am going to give myself permission for .... minutes a week

on .... (day) at .... (time) to be creative.

I am going to try the following ways to do this:

1. ....

2. ....

3. ....

(e) **The Word of God**

You may remember we did some work on thinking about which particular way of experiencing the Word of God most nourished you. Perhaps this was a new way for you that you had not much explored before. You may like to decide you are going to continue to explore God's Word in a new way.

On the course my preferred ways of hearing the Word of God

were: ....

....

I am now going to try and develop this by ....

....

(f) **Intercessory prayer**

You will remember that we did a session that looked out into the world around us. It used maps and current newspapers, amongst other things. Perhaps there was some point of interest that you found in that session that you want to keep on using.

- Perhaps a particular area in the world.
- Perhaps using your daily newspaper for prayer.

- Perhaps gathering maps and other information about some work in God's world for which you want to pray regularly.

I want to pray for God's world in the following specific ways:

I am interested in praying for God's world by ....

....

My times of prayer for it will be ....

....

(g) **Believing**

In the session on Believing we encouraged people to explore their doubts and their faith journey to their present place of belief. You might want to keep working on this area. You might want to do more reading or join a discussion group or attend some Christian gathering that deals with a particular area of believing.

My main point of interest in my quest for a deeper faith is ....

....

I want to pursue this more by doing..

....

(h) **Forgiveness**

In the course we touched on issues of forgiveness and the patterning of our life; whom we relate to and how. You may feel that this is an area you want to take further.

My main relationships which need development are ....

....

I intend to do this about them in the future...............................

....